IMAGES
of America

BANNERMAN CASTLE

IMAGES
of America

BANNERMAN CASTLE

Thom Johnson and Barbara H. Gottlock

ARCADIA
PUBLISHING

Published by Arcadia Publishing
Charleston SC, Chicago IL, Portsmouth NH, San Francisco CA

Printed in the United States of America

Library of Congress Catalog Card Number: 2006928532

For all general information contact Arcadia Publishing at:
Telephone 843-853-2070
Fax 843-853-0044
E-mail sales@arcadiapublishing.com
For customer service and orders:
Toll-Free 1-888-313-2665

Visit us on the Internet at www.arcadiapublishing.com

This is Francis Bannerman VI in his office at 501 Broadway, New York City. The authors dedicate this book to him and his Museum of Lost Arts. It was his hope that his military collection would lead to the study of war so that the world would no longer have to practice it. (From Francis Bannerman Sons catalog.)

CONTENTS

Acknowledgments   6

Introduction   7

1.   Pollepel Island   9

2.   The Business Begins   15

3.   The Island Solves a Problem   27

4.   The Construction Years, 1901–1918   33

5.   The Island Workers   63

6.   Helen Bannerman and Sons   73

7.   The Decline and the Shutdown   85

8.   From Island to Parkland   101

9.   The Bannerman Castle Trust   111

Epilogue   119

ACKNOWLEDGMENTS

The authors would like to thank the following for their help with this project: Val Forgett III, Jane Bannerman, the Hagley Library and Museum, Neil Caplan and the Bannerman Castle Trust, Patrick DiBenedetto, Adam Farber, Paul Harrington, Brian Lavey, Jan Novak, Jim Logan, Robert "Raccoon" Lynch, Gary Ferguson, Dorothea G. Bannerman, Heidi M. Churchill, Jeffrey B. Churchill, the New York Public Library, the Cornell University Library, Sheldon Stowe, the Jackson Hole Preserve, Mel Johnson and the Staff at Washington's Headquarters in Newburgh, Mike Khantzian, Bill Diamond, the Leonard Wayne Owen family, Larry Simpkins, Rob Yasinsac, and especially Wes Gottlock for getting the kinks out.

INTRODUCTION

History is defined as "the branch of knowledge dealing with past events." In the hope for the resurrection of Bannerman Castle, it is important to know its basic story in order to realize the value of its history in the plan of things. Thanks go to the imaginative work of Neil Caplan for setting a rescue in motion with the Bannerman Castle Trust. With the cooperation of the New York State Office of Parks, Recreation and Historical Preservation, as well as volunteers who have given many hours of hard work, the castle will regain its place in the historic Hudson for all to see. Now Thom Johnson and Barbara Gottlock have put together this fine book with pictures from the past to set the scene for the future. The whole Bannerman family supports this work. Well done!

—Jane Campbell Bannerman, Spring 2006

Carved from glaciers thousands of feet thick during the last Ice Age, the majestic Hudson Highlands straddle the Hudson River from Haverstraw Bay north to Newburgh Bay. At the northern end of this natural fiord, about 1,000 feet from the river's eastern shore in the town of Fishkill, lies a small island. Despite its modest size of 6.5 acres, the island's rich history is accompanied by legend, mystery, and intrigue.

The island is known locally as Bannerman's Island but its official designation is Pollepel Island. The actual derivation of the name Pollepel (variant spellings: Polopel, Polipel, Pollipel, Pollopel, Polypus) is not known, although there are several possible explanations for it. The stories behind these theories will be illustrated in chapter 1.

Native tribes cohabited (not always in a friendly manner) in the region for hundreds of years. However, the course of history took a sudden turn when Henry Hudson sailed in 1609. While searching for a northwest passage to India, Hudson provided the first glimpses into the area around Pollepel. The *Half Moon*'s logs describe many encounters with the natives of the area, probably of Algonquin origin. Some relics of native activity on the island have been found, but it is believed that the island may have been used primarily as a defensive outpost or lookout point. Paradoxically legend has it that some native tribes thought the island to be haunted and Pollepel became a safe haven for their enemies.

As Dutch exploration expanded, their own superstitions surrounding Pollepel grew as well. Legends abound about the Heer of Dunderberg and his mysterious goblins. It has been written that Dutch sailors were terrified by the eerie howling winds resonating through the Hudson Highlands as their ships sailed northward toward Pollepel. Adding to their fears, the echoing claps of thunder reverberating between the highlands's steep walls and bolts of lightning illuminating the valley's night were deemed to be the work of some evil force. The Heer and his demonic cohorts were held responsible. Newer sailors, legend has it, were ceremoniously dunked in the waters around Pollepel. This process served to "immunize" the sailors against any further wrath from the Heer. Pollepel was considered the northernmost boundary of the Heer's influence. Once past the island, the waters smoothed and the horrors diminished.

In the 17th and early 18th centuries, fur trading flourished as the Dutch and British vied for control of the Hudson River Valley. Eventually the British prevailed, but events leading up to 1776 changed all of that.

The Hudson Highlands became a strategic focal point of Revolutionary War battles. Pollepel Island played an interesting role in America's defense of the highlands. Maj. Gen. Philip Schuyler urged the New York State Convention to thwart British ship movement north through the Hudson. He proposed the construction of a cheveaux-de-frise across the river stretching from Pollepel Island to Plum Point on the western bank. Under the engineering direction of Capt. Thomas Machin, log frames of 40 by 45 feet were sunk at 15 foot intervals across the river. The frames were then weighted down with stones. Long, slanted beams with sharp iron points extended upward to just below the water's surface, threatening the hulls of invading British ships.

In October 1777, a British fleet passed through the obstructions with surprising ease much to the chagrin of American officers. Several theories have been offered for the obstruction's failure. Some believe the obstruction in fact had not been completed since resources were being diverted to the chain link across the Hudson at West Point. Others surmise that traitors to the American cause may have informed British officers of the location of a narrow passage left open in the cheveaux-de-frise to enable river traffic to flow. Another theory has either the traitors or the British themselves dismantling one of the beams.

In 1781, plans to build a military prison and a munitions storage facility on Pollepel Island were offered by Maj. Gen. William Heath. With Gen. George Washington's approval, construction of the prison began on the island's south side. However, there is no evidence the prison was ever finished. With the war winding down, perhaps a decision was made to abandon the project. A stone wall still stands on the south end of the island that marks the prison's proposed site.

After the Revolution, Pollepel Island became little more than a recreational destination. Those willing to boat across the tricky waters enjoyed swimming, picnicking, fishing, and parties. Various temporary buildings or sheds were built on the island during the 19th century. Shad fishermen, including members of the Henry Ward Beecher family, constructed sheds on the island.

Not all was idyllic however. Eventually the island became a haven for some undesirables. Bootleggers sold their goods there to avoid paying taxes. Rumors of prostitution persisted. Around that time, Matthew Vassar sought to use Pollepel Island as a location for a monument dedicated to Henry Hudson to commemorate his discovery of the Hudson River. He failed to garner the necessary support and the effort was abandoned. The funds set aside for the monument instead went towards the establishment of Vassar College. In 1888, Mary Taft bought the island to put a permanent halt to the proliferation of vices. Ownership was eventually passed to Francis Bannerman VI in 1900.

The life of Francis Bannerman VI presents a fascinating journey. In the mid-19th century, young Bannerman and his family were not much different than thousands of other immigrants seeking to assimilate and to find a better life. His business life began humbly enough. Using a grappling hook to gather and resell scrap from the Brooklyn Navy Yard, Bannerman's business continued to evolve and grow in ways he probably never imagined. He eventually became the country's preeminent purveyor of military goods. For reasons to be shown in this book, the bulk of his massive collection eventually found its way to Pollepel Island.

Not content to construct mundane facilities for his goods on the island, Bannerman set out to design and build a series of unique structures from influences he gleaned during his world travels. Although he was not a trained architect, his hand-drawn sketches were detailed enough for his work crews to begin work on the Bannerman Castle complex. Construction continued on the island until his death in 1918.

The ensuing chapters will show the story of Pollepel Island once it passed into Bannerman's hands. He was a complex man whose ingenuity, creativity, and industry left behind a remarkable legacy. The enchanting castle complex he constructed on the island served a dual purpose. Not only did the structures serve his business needs, they also created a visual spectacle and a source of wonder and inspiration to generations.

—Wes Gottlock

One

POLLEPEL ISLAND

The derivation of the name Pollepel is not known, although there are several possible explanations. The first is that the island was named after the polypus cactus, which once grew abundantly on the island. Although it no longer grows on the island, some may be found on nearby Breakneck Ridge.

Another explanation has the Dutch calling the island Pollepel after their word for "ladle." Tales exist of freshmen sailors who were drunk or who misbehaved while on board. The recalcitrants would be dropped off on the island to await the ship's return. These sailors, hopefully sober and wiser, would then be scooped up using a device that resembled a ladle.

A third possible derivative is that the name came from an Indian word meaning "divider of the waters."

On the next page, the story of Polly Pell will illustrate the final possible explanation. Although several versions exist, the central theme remains the same.

Whatever the origin of the name, Pollepel Island was owned by several people before Francis Bannerman VI purchased it on December 5, 1900. The first deed was granted June 17, 1697, to Adolph Philipse. It was part of the Highland Patent of Adolph Philipse. At the time of the Revolutionary War it was owned by Philip Philipse and his sisters Mary Morris, wife of Col. Roger Morris, and Susannah Robinson, wife of Beverly Robinson. Since the Morris and Robinson families were loyalists, the property was confiscated and sold to William Van Wyck of Fishkill by Daniel Graham as commissioner of forfeitures of the State of New York on June 23, 1788. The property then passed into the hands of Walter C. Anthony for a very short time in February 1888. Anthony then sold the island to Mary G. Taft of Cornwall on February 11, 1888. Taft sold the island to Francis Bannerman VI on December 5, 1900.

One explanation for the island's name is the story of Polly Pell. Polly Pell was a local farmer's daughter. She was betrothed to the Reverend Paul Vernon but she really loved Guert Brinkerhoff. Brinkerhoff was jealous of the reverend and therefore he would follow Pell and the reverend wherever they went. One winter day Brinkerhoff heard that the reverend was taking Pell on a sleigh ride on the frozen Hudson River. Brinkerhoff warned them of the danger of thin ice but they paid him no heed. Once again Brinkerhoff followed them and sure enough the ice broke and the sleigh with its passengers fell into the river. Brinkerhoff leapt into the icy water and after a considerable struggle, he managed to get the reverend and Pell safely onto a piece of pancake ice. The ice floated and eventually landed on an island in the river. As soon as they landed Pell threw her arms around Brinkerhoff. The reverend, seeing Pell's love for Brinkerhoff and knowing she did not love him, married them on the spot. The next morning Brinkerhoff swam ashore and brought back one of the family's servants to row them home. The servant named the island Polly Pell's Island. (Drawing by Bill Diamond.)

The polypus cactus shown in the foreground of this photograph grew on Pollepel Island at one time. The island might be named for it. This cactus still grows on Breakneck Ridge, which is very near the island. (Photograph by Margaret Santangelo.)

In this sketch, Dutch sailors are rescued by the "pollepel," a Dutch word for ladle. It is a possible explanation for the name of the island. (Drawing by Bill Diamond.)

This map, drawn by Capt. Thomas Machin on January 4, 1778, shows the island, spelled "Polapis." Note the proposed path of the cheveaux-de-frise from Pollepel Island to Plum Point, on the western shore of the Hudson River. Machin also marked the placement of fortifications on the island and the surrounding shores. There is no evidence that the fortifications were ever actually placed on the island. (Courtesy of the Division of Rare and Manuscript Collections, Cornell University Library.)

The cheveaux-de-frise stretching across the Hudson River from Pollepel Island to Plum Point, was a tactical failure. It is still unclear if it was ever completed. The construction of the chain barriers across the river at West Point may have diverted manpower and materials needed to complete the cheveaux-de-frise. (Drawing by Wes Gottlock.)

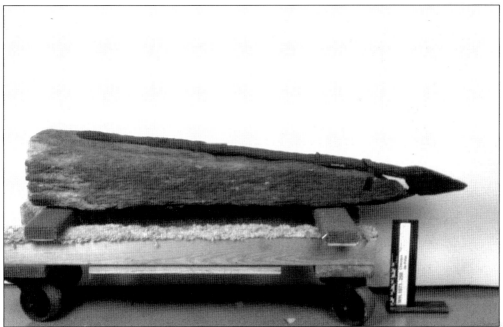

The photograph above shows the only portion of the cheveaux-de-frise ever recovered from the Hudson River. In 1828 or 1836, Capt. Abraham Elting pulled up this point and partial beam while his sloop was anchored near Pollepel Island. It was eventually sold to Abraham Tomlinson who, in turn, sold it to Enoch Carter, curator at Washington's Headquarters in Newburgh in 1856. (Courtesy of Washington's Headquarters State Historic Site, New York State Office of Parks, Recreation and Historic Preservation.)

The legendary Heer of Dunderberg wreaks havoc on a ship sailing up the Hudson River. Once past Pollepel Island, the sailors were deemed safe. (Drawing by Bill Diamond.)

This is a view looking north up the Hudson River. Storm King Station is in the foreground. Pollepel Island can be seen in the distance before Bannerman built any structures on it. (Courtesy of the Robert N. Dennis Collection of Stereoscopic Views, Miriam and Ira D. Wallach Division of Art, Prints and Photographs, the New York Public Library, Astor, Lenox and Tilden Foundations.)

Two

THE BUSINESS BEGINS

Francis Bannerman VI was born in Dundee, Scotland, on March 24, 1851, to Francis Bannerman V and Margaret McWalter. Francis V's father arrived in New York on August 14, 1854, aboard the *Constitution*. His wife Margaret and their three children, Jane, 11; Francis, 3; and James, 11 months; followed aboard the *Constantine* on October 2, 1854. The family lived in New Jersey for a short time before settling in Brooklyn. Francis V made his living in a variety of ways but ended up selling surplus material found in and around the Brooklyn Navy Yard.

When the Civil War started, Bannerman V joined the Union Army. His son was forced to quit school and go to work to help support the family. Using an old anchor as a grappling hook, he retrieved rope and other material from the New York harbor.

By the time his father returned from the war Francis had accumulated so much surplus material that he and his father began what many consider to be the first army-navy store.

In 1871, Francis Bannerman VI, with his father's blessing, started his own business. Although the business was in direct competition with his father's, the elder Bannerman felt it would be beneficial for both of them in the long run.

In 1872, Francis VI traveled to Ireland looking for rope, which was in short supply in the United States. While there he met Helen Boyce and married her on June 8, 1872. According to Francis's will, he and Helen had a prenuptial agreement stating "the results financially of our joint efforts be shared equally." When they returned from Ireland in October 1872, Francis opened his first store at 43 Atlantic Avenue in Brooklyn. The business sold apples, potatoes, and other produce in addition to the hardware and goods that he purchased at government auctions.

New locations were acquired to accommodate the growing needs of his business. Operations were moved to New York City at 118 Broad Street, 27 Front Street, and 579 Broadway, before finally settling at 501 Broadway as its main headquarters. The building at 501 Broadway was purchased from the Metropolitan Museum of Art on June 29, 1905. The company name was Francis Bannerman Sons Inc.

Before Francis Bannerman VI achieved great success in the trading of military surplus, the family owned and operated several humble businesses. By 1890, records show Bannerman businesses at three locations (14 Atlantic Street, 1572 Bergen Street, and 1114 Butler, all in Brooklyn). (Courtesy of Hagley Museum and Library.)

Brooklyn, Sept 20 1878

M _Bannerman_

Bought of M. BANNERMAN,

WHOLESALE

POTATOE DEALER,

No. 14 ATLANTIC STREET.

Potatoes constantly on hand from the Northern and Western parts of New York State, Jackson Whites, Prince Alberts, Peerless, Red and White Peach Blows and early Rose for seed and Domestic use.

☞ My Motto is, Quick Sales and Small Profits. ☜

435
473
412
520
347
295
159
2641

503
510
270
510
1793

2641 ℔ Lines @ 4⅜	11 5 54	
	47.06	
1793 ℔ Gear Rope 2⅝		
361 . Reef Points @ 3ᵈ	10 8 3	

Lines new 59 ℔ short
Gear Rope 32.

The Bannermans are listed as potato dealers on this 1878 bill of sale. Oddly enough, the purchase was for rope. (Courtesy of Hagley Museum and Library.)

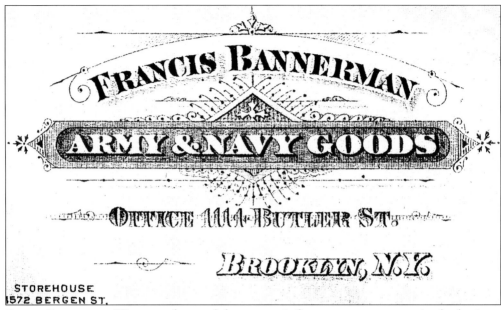

FRANCIS BANNERMAN

ARMY & NAVY GOODS

OFFICE 1114 BUTLER ST.

BROOKLYN, N.Y.

STOREHOUSE
1572 BERGEN ST.

Francis Bannerman VI operated one of the country's first army-navy stores. As the business grew and evolved, Bannerman bought a building at 501 Broadway. It was purchased from the Metropolitan Museum of Art on June 29, 1905. With its amazing array of merchandise, the store became a mecca for collectors during its years at Broadway and Spring Street. The building would remain the heart of the business until the late 1950s when it was no longer economically viable to operate. (Courtesy of Hagley Museum and Library.)

TELEPHONE	ESTABLISHED	CABLE ADDRESS
1754 SPRING	1865	BANNERMAN, N. Y.

FRANCIS BANNERMAN

ORDNANCE

WAR RELICS

MILITARY GOODS

501 BROADWAY, NEW YORK, U. S. A.

CATALOGUE

—OF—

GUNS, SWORDS, CANNONS,

EQUIPMENTS,

—AND—

MILITARY GOODS,

—FOR SALE BY—

FRANCIS BANNERMAN,

1114 Butler St.,

BROOKLYN, N. Y.

———————●———————

OCTOBER, 1888.

H. N. Atkinson, Printer, 82 Wall Street, N. Y.

Bannerman's first catalog was published in 1884. It was handwritten. This 1888 catalog was the first printed one. It contained 12 pages. Items included rifles, revolvers, saddles, swords, cartridges, belts, and cannons. Eventually several editions of the world wide catalog would exceed 300 pages. (From Francis Bannerman Sons 1888 catalog.)

THIS CATALOGUE

Supercedes all Previous Issues.

—TERMS.——

As most of the goods offered in this catalogue have been purchased from the Government, who sell only for cash, it becomes necessary for me to adopt the same rule. Therefore, terms are

Spot Cash.

All Prices Quoted are Net Prices.

Goods will be delivered free of charge for cartage, to railroad, steamboat or express, in New York City.

All goods will be at the risk of purchaser after shipment from New York.

No charge for packing cases.

All goods are quoted, if on hand when order is received.

In ordering lots quoted as **REFINISHED,** *it will be necessary to allow time to have them sent to the armory.*

All claims must be made within three days after receipt of goods; otherwise they will not be entertained.

Any Part of a lot will be Sold at Price Quoted.

When the whole quantity in any lot is taken, five per cent. discount will be allowed.

Goods will be shipped C. O. D., upon receipt of sufficient amount to pay express charges both ways. and goods will then be sent: " Privelege to examine." less the amount remitted.

→ PAYMENTS. ←

Remittances may be made by **Check, Draft,** *or* **Post Office Order.** **Stamps** *taken for sums less than $1.00. Money should always be sent by registered mail.*

Electrotypes of cuts in this Catalogue can be furnished at $1.00 each.

The inside cover of the April 1889 catalog set forth Bannerman's terms of purchase. Note particularly his requirement of "spot cash." (From Francis Bannerman Sons 1889 catalog.)

RELICS.

COLLECTION OF 50 DIFFERENT KINDS OF ARMS.

AS USED BY THE U. S. GOVT. LAST 75 YEARS.

List on application.   All in fine order, having been refinished.   Price, $300.00

A Collecti n of 15 Different Kinds of Revolvers and Pistols,

Used by U. S Government, last 40 Years.

List on application.   All in fine Order, having been refinished.   Price, $75.00

A Collection of Bombshells, as Used in Civil War.

List on application.   Free from Powder.   Total weight, 1,500 lbs.   Price for lot, $100

6 Swords, as used by the U. S. Cavalry, 1840, straight blades, in good
   refinished order.   .   .   .   .   Price, each,   2.50

1000 Flints for flint lock muskets and pistols   .   .   .   Each, .05

25 Dragon Horse Pistols with extension stocks; primer locks; in fine order,
   swiveled ramrod. Cal. 58.   .   .   .   .   Each, 2.50

Lot of 50 Assorted Rifles, Muskets and Carbines, part of the lot surrendered
   by the Indian Chief, Sitting Bull, to the U.S. Government, after the Custer
   Massacre; some of the rifles are the Leman Indian Sporting Rifle with
   heavy barrels and fine sights; stocks and woodwork are worn thin; some
   stocks are repaired with buckskin; some are still loaded. Charges will be
   withdrawn before shipment. Prices: Carbines, $3; muskets, $4; sporting
   rifles, $5; some Henry Repeating Rifles in lot.   .   .   Price, $7.00

Signature of Patrick Henry, to a Land Grant,

With the Seal of the Commonwealth of Virginia, A. D. 1783.   Price, $100.00

Reindeer Skin Fur Coats

WITH HOODS.

Made for use of the Greeley Relief Expedition; no style, but lots of comfort in cold
   weather; reindeer skins have thickest fur known; flesh side is nicely alum
   or Indian tanned.   .   .   .   .   .   Price, $10.00

100 Pair Greeley Rubber Sandals purchased from U. S. Navy on the return of
   the Greeley Relief Expedition from Arctic regions; sizes very large—10s, 12s
   and 14s, new, with heel strap and buckles; useful in cold weather.   Price, .75

10 Sleeping Bags of Elk or Reindeer Skin,

Six feet long, with flaps and buttons, new, from Greeley relief expedition,
   Price, $15.00

5000 Lbs. Pemmican Prepared Meat.

Put up by Kemp, Day & Co. of New York, for the Greeley relief Exhibition; will
   keep for 20 years.   Packed in 1½ and 7 lb cans.   Price, 10 cents per lb.

This page from the April 1889 catalog illustrates the great variety of goods available. Of unique interest are the signature of Patrick Henry, reindeer skin fur coats and sleeping bags, and 5,000 pounds of pemmican prepared meat. Pemmican is dried lean meat, pounded into a paste with fat and preserved in the form of pressed cakes. (From Francis Bannerman Sons 1889 catalog.)

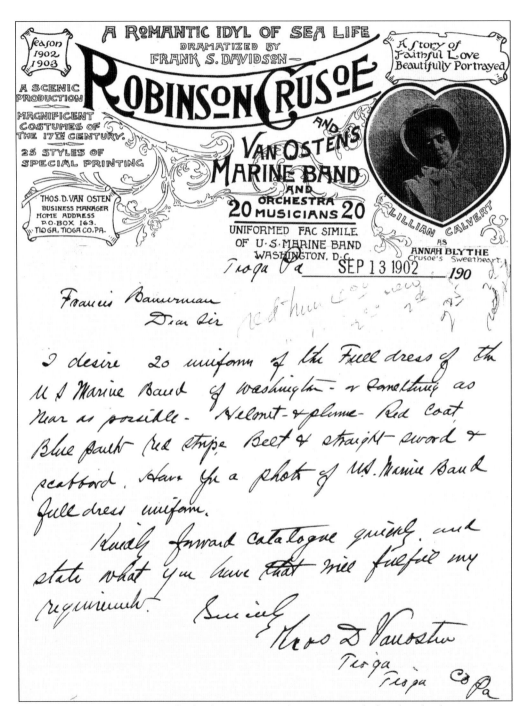

A ROMANTIC IDYL OF SEA LIFE
DRAMATIZED BY FRANK S. DAVIDSON

Season 1902 1903

ROBINSON CRUSOE

A SCENIC PRODUCTION

MAGNIFICENT COSTUMES OF THE 17TH CENTURY.

25 STYLES OF SPECIAL PRINTING

THOS. D. VAN OSTEN
BUSINESS MANAGER
HOME ADDRESS
P.O. BOX 163.
TIOGA, TIOGA CO. PA.

AND VAN OSTEN'S MARINE BAND AND ORCHESTRA
20 MUSICIANS 20

UNIFORMED FAC SIMILE OF U·S·MARINE BAND WASHINGTON, D.C.

A Story of Faithful Love Beautifully Portrayed

LILLIAN CALVERT

AS ANNAH BLYTHE Crusoe's Sweetheart.

Tioga Pa _____ SEP 13 1902 _____ 190

Francis Bannerman
Dear Sir

I desire 20 uniforms of the Full dress of the U S Marine Band of washington — or something as near as possible — Helmet — & plume — Red Coat Blue pants (red stripe Belt & straight sword & scabbord. Have you a photo of U.S. Marine Band full dress uniform.

Kindly forward catalogue quickly. and state what you have that will fulfil my requirements.

Sincerely
Thos D VanOsten
Tioga
Tioga Co Pa

The Bannerman business supplied a diverse range of customers including bands, theater groups, circus performers, rodeos, movie producers, and vaudeville acts in addition to military goods collectors. The Bannerman catalog was a valuable resource for many. (Courtesy of the Hagley Museum and Library.)

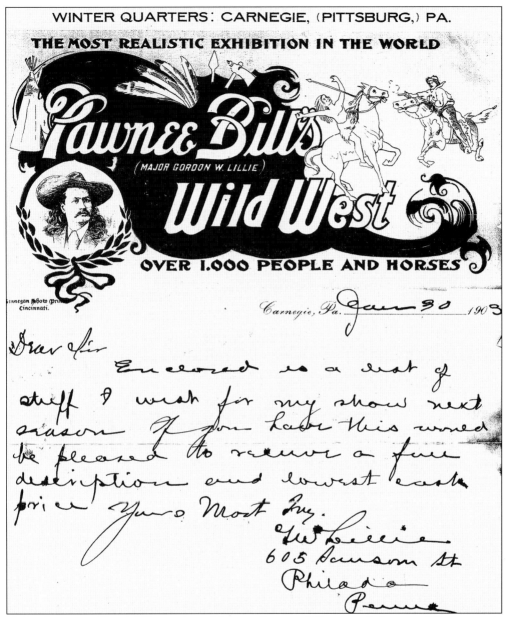

WINTER QUARTERS: CARNEGIE, (PITTSBURG,) PA.

THE MOST REALISTIC EXHIBITION IN THE WORLD

Pawnee Bill's
(MAJOR GORDON W. LILLIE)
Wild West

OVER 1,000 PEOPLE AND HORSES

Carnegie, Pa. Jan 30 1903

Dear Sir

Enclosed is a list of stuff I wish for my show next season If you have this would be pleased to receive a full description and lowest cash price Yours Most Try.

Lillie
605 Ransom St
Phila
Penn

To outfit many of his 1,000 people and horses, Pawnee Bill required the use of Bannerman's services. Other entertainers included the Marvelous Le Barons—America's Greatest Contortionists; Charles Lee's Royal Circus, Menagerie, and Museum of Wonder; Indian Bill's Historic Wild West Indian Museum; Hyde and Heath singers and comedians (who ordered first class officer's uniforms and fatigues coats, all size 34); Stevens Stock Theatrical Company (who ordered confederate coats and trousers); and Broncho John's Realistic Western Amusement Enterprises. (Courtesy of the Hagley Museum and Library.)

After starting his own business in 1871, Francis Bannerman VI opened his first store at 43 Atlantic Avenue, Brooklyn. As his inventory of material grew, Bannerman moved the operation to this store at 118 Broad Street in Manhattan (shown in the picture). Note the use of flags, both patriotic and commercial. Later American flags would be prominently displayed all over Pollepel Island. (From Francis Bannerman Sons catalog.)

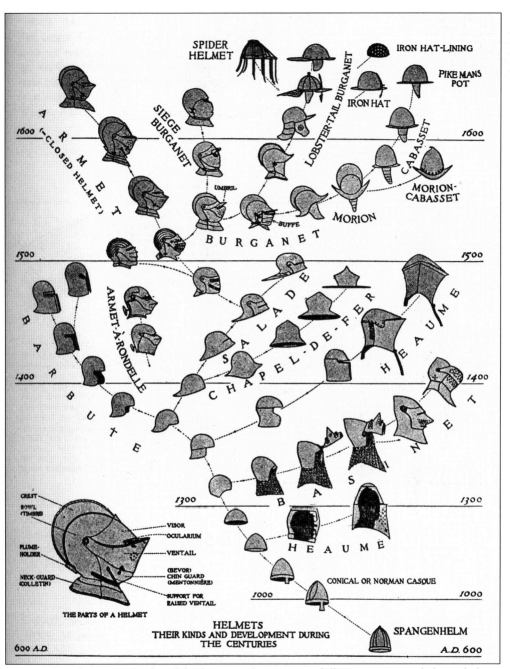

SPIDER HELMET

IRON HAT-LINING

PIKE MANS POT

SIEGE BURGANET

LOBSTER-TAIL BURGANET

IRON HAT

CABASSET

ARMET (-CLOSED HELMET)

MORION-CABASSET

UMBRIL

MORION

BUFFE

BURGANET

1600 — 1600

1500 — 1500

SALADE

ARMET-Á-RONDELLE

CHAPEL-DE-FER

HEAUME

BASINET

BARBUTE

1400 — 1400

1300 — 1300

HEAUME

CREST
BOWL (TIMBRE)
VISOR
OCULARIUM
PLUME-HOLDER
VENTAIL
(BEVOR)
CHIN GUARD (MENTONNIÈRE)
NECK-GUARD (COLLETIN)
SUPPORT FOR RAISED VENTAIL

CONICAL OR NORMAN CASQUE

1000 — 1000

THE PARTS OF A HELMET

HELMETS
THEIR KINDS AND DEVELOPMENT DURING
THE CENTURIES

SPANGENHELM

600 A.D. — A.D. 600

Often the catalogs contained useful reference information and illustrations intended to enlighten the reader. In the 1966 100th anniversary edition, this chart shows the styles and development of helmets through the centuries. Note the time line. (From Francis Bannerman Sons catalog)

25

The interior of 501 Broadway displayed an enormous range of material that was offered for sale. Browsers were welcome to explore the floors of merchandise. The Museum of Lost Arts, located on the upper two floors, had wide appeal to collectors and history buffs. Visitors could examine war relics from the stone age to World War I. (From Francis Bannerman Sons catalog.)

Three

The Island Solves
a Problem

When Francis Bannerman VI completed the purchase of most of the military goods after the Spanish-American War in 1898, he probably had no plans for storage. As his Brooklyn warehouse filled with this material, he found that he had a major problem—how to safely store his large stock of black powder. His neighbors were not happy with this potentially dangerous material being stored near their homes and businesses. The solution to the problem would be a little island up the Hudson River near West Point.

There are two versions explaining how Pollepel Island was chosen. One version told by Francis Bannerman VI to the Men's League of the Cornwall-on-Hudson Presbyterian Church on September 2, 1915, is that he spotted the island during an excursion aboard a Hudson River Dayliner and later sent his son David to investigate. Another story maintains that David and his friend, Daniel Carver, saw the island while canoeing on the Hudson River.

After learning that the island was owned by Mary Taft, Bannerman approached her so he could buy it from her. The deed that Bannerman and Taft agreed on included a covenant that Bannerman and his heirs "shall not manufacture or sell or expose for sale any malt, spirituous or intoxicating liquor whatever as a beverage or drink in, about or upon the premises." Bannerman had no problem with that stipulation given that he was in favor of prohibition.

The island was sold to Bannerman on December 5, 1900, for $600 cash with Mary Taft holding a mortgage of $1,000 to be paid over two to three years, at the rate of 5.5 percent. In the spring of 1901, he contracted a firm from Beacon to build two structures on the island—a three floored arsenal on the northeast corner of the island, and a small two story superintendent's house near the arsenal. Island rock was blasted down to just above the high water mark to create a level area for construction. A small dock was also created at the northeast side near the front of the arsenal. He had not built a castle, just an arsenal. The castle would start in 1905.

Warranty Deed.

Mary G. Taft
to
Francis Bannerman

Dated Dec. 5, 1900.
Ackn. Dec. 5 1900.
Rec'd. Dec. 10, 1900
Liber 309 of Deeds
page 498.

Consideration $600.00 Conveys same premises by same description. Covenant against manufacture or sale of liquor on premises.

Mortgage.

Francis Bannerman
and Nellie B. Bannerman
his wife,
to
Mary G. Taft.

Dated Dec. 6, 1900.
Ackn. Dec. 6 1900.
Rec'd. Dec. 10, 1900
Liber 249 Mortgs.
page 373

Secures $1000.00 Purchase money mortgage. Covers same premises and by the same description as set forth in above deeds.

Charles S. Williams,
Counsellor at Law,
39 Cortlandt St. New York City

Wyko

This deed shows the transfer of Pollepel Island from Mary G. Taft to Francis Bannerman on December 5, 1900. The covenant against the manufacture or sale of liquor is written in the center of the document. The island was purchased for $600 cash with a $1,000 mortgage. Bannerman began construction in the spring of 1901. (Courtesy of the Hagley Museum and Library.)

In 1901, Frances Bannerman began the construction of the superintendent's house on the northern end of the island. The above photograph (looking south) shows a construction shed built to house materials. In the photograph below, the superintendent's house (on the right) nears completion. It would later be modified to accommodate the building of the No. 3 Arsenal. (Courtesy of the Churchill/Bannerman family.)

This illustration shows the No. 1 Arsenal and dock as they appeared in 1901. The east side provided the entrance to the building. There were loading doors in the center of each floor. There is evidence that the dock was at the northeast corner and at an odd angle to the arsenal. It was designed to resemble the entrance of the Spenser Factory in Brooklyn, and because of this island workers often referred to it as the Spenser building. (Illustration by Thom Johnson.)

Shown here is the No. 1 Arsenal as it looked in 1901. To the right is the superintendent's house with its front entrance facing north. By 1905, the space between the buildings was filled in by the No. 3 Arsenal and the North Gate. (Illustration by Thom Johnson.)

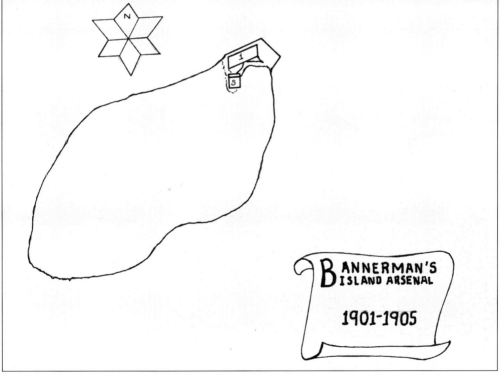

In this postcard labeled "North Gate of Highlands from N., Hudson River, N.Y.," the No. 1 Arsenal on Pollepel Island is clearly visible. This postcard was printed by the Valentine and Sons Publishing Company.

BANNERMAN'S ISLAND ARSENAL

1901-1905

This plan shows the No. 1 Arsenal in the shape of a parallelogram. It is unknown why Bannerman designed the building without right angles at the corners. It is possible that he believed the building appeared larger that way. When he whitewashed the walls and painted the business name and address, the billboard would seem more prominent. The other shape in the plan shows the superintendent's house. (Plans by Thom Johnson.)

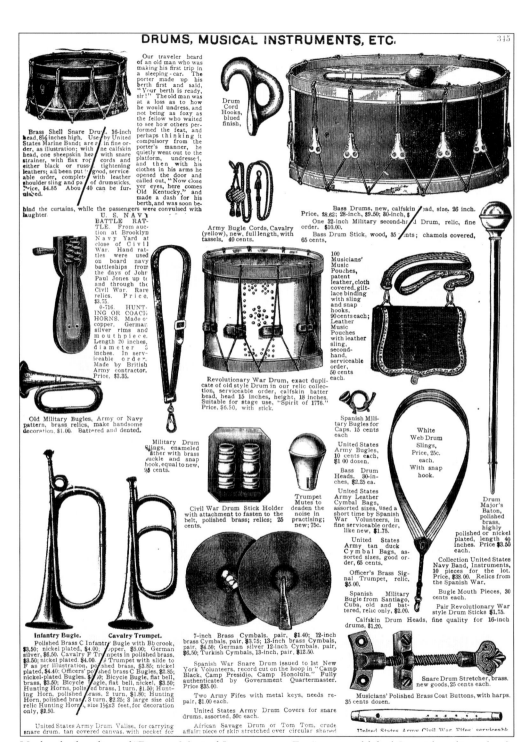

Brass Shell Snare Drum, 16-inch head, 8½ inches high. Used by United States Marine Band; are in fine order, as illustration; with the calfskin head, one sheepskin head with snare strainer, with flax rope cords and either black or russet tightening leathers; all been put in good, serviceable order, complete with leather shoulder sling and pair of drumsticks. Price, $4.85. About 40 can be furnished.

Our traveler heard of an old man who was making his first trip in a sleeping - car. The porter made up his berth first and said, "Your berth is ready, sir!" The old man was at a loss as to how he would undress, and not being as foxy as the fellow who waited to see how others performed the feat, and perhaps thinking it compulsory from the porter's manner, he quietly went out to the platform, undressed, and then with his clothes in his arms he opened the door and called out, "Now close yer eyes, here comes Old Kentucky," and made a dash for his berth, and was soon behind the curtains, while the passengers were convulsed with laughter.

Drum Cord Hooks, blued finish.

Bass Drums, new, calfskin head, size, 26 inch. Price, $8.62; 28-inch, $9.50; 30-inch, $ One 32-inch Military second-hand Drum, relic, fine order. $10.00.
Bass Drum Stick, wood, 35 cents; chamois covered, 65 cents.

U. S. NAVY BATTLE RATTLE: From auction at Brooklyn Navy Yard at close of Civil War. Hand rattles were used on board navy battleships from the days of John Paul Jones up to and through the Civil War. Rare relics. Price, $3.75.

0-716. HUNTING OR COACH HORNS. Made of copper, German silver rims and mouthpiece. Length 20 inches, diameter 5 inches. In serviceable order. Made by British Army contractor. Price, $3.35.

Army Bugle Cords, Cavalry (yellow), new, full length, with tassels. 40 cents.

100 Musicians' Music Pouches, patent leather, cloth covered, gilt-lace binding with sling and snap hooks, 90 cents each; Leather Music Pouches with leather sling, second-hand, serviceable order, 50 cents each.

Old Military Bugles, Army or Navy pattern, brass relics, make handsome decoration, $1.00. Battered and dented.

Military Drum Slings, enameled leather with brass buckle and snap hook, equal to new, 95 cents.

Revolutionary War Drum, exact duplicate of old style Drum in our relic collection, serviceable order, calfskin batter head, head 15 inches, height, 18 inches. Suitable for stage use, "Spirit of 1776." Price, $6.50, with stick.

Spanish Military Bugles for Caps, 15 cents each
United States Army Bugles, 10 cents each, $1.00 dozen.
Bass Drum Heads, 30-inches, $2.25 ea.

White Web Drum Slings, Price, 25c. each. With snap hook.

Trumpet Mutes to deaden the noise in practising; new; 75c.

United States Army Leather Cymbal Bags, assorted sizes, used a short time by Spanish War Volunteers, in fine serviceable order, like new, $1.75.

United States Army tan duck Cymbal Bags, assorted sizes, good order, 65 cents.

Officer's Brass Signal Trumpet, relic. $5.00.

Spanish Military Bugle from Santiago, Cuba, old and battered, relic only, $2.00.

Calfskin Drum Heads, fine quality for 16-inch drums, $1.20.

Drum Major's Baton, polished brass, highly polished or nickel plated, length 40 inches. Price $3.50 each.

Collection United States Navy Band, Instruments, 10 pieces for the lot. Price, $38.00. Relics from the Spanish War.

Bugle Mouth Pieces, 30 cents each.

Pair Revolutionary War style Drum Sticks $1.75.

Civil War Drum Stick Holder with attachment to fasten to the belt, polished brass; relics; 25 cents.

Infantry Bugle.
Polished Brass C Infantry Bugle with Bb crook, $3.50; nickel plated, $4.00. German silver, $6.50. Cavalry F Trumpets in polished brass, $3.50; nickel plated, $4.00.

Cavalry Trumpet.
Trumpet with slide to F as per illustration, polished brass, $3.85; nickel plated, $4.40; Officers' polished brass C Bugles, $2.85; nickel-plated Bugles. $ 10; Bicycle Bugle, flat bell, brass, $3.50; Bicycle Bugle, flat bell, nickel, $3.50; Hunting Horns, polished brass, 1 turn, $1.50; Hunting Horn, polished brass, 2 turn, $1.80; Hunting Horn, polished brass, 3 turn, $2.25; 3 large size old relic Hunting Horn, size 1½x3 feet, for decoration only, $2.50.

United States Army Drum Valise, for carrying snare drum, tan covered canvas, with pocket for

7-inch Brass Cymbals, pair, $1.40; 12-inch brass Cymbals, pair, $3.75; 13-inch brass Cymbals, pair, $4.50; German silver 12-inch Cymbals, pair, $6.50; Turkish Cymbals, 13-inch, pair, $12.50.

Spanish War Snare Drum issued to 1st New York Volunteers, record cut on the hoop in "Camp Black, Camp Presidio, Camp Honolulu." Fully authenticated by Government Quartermaster. Price $35.00.

Two Army Fifes with metal keys, needs repair, $1.00 each.

United States Army Drum Covers for snare drums, assorted, 50c each.

African Savage Drum or Tom Tom, crude affair; piece of skin stretched over circular shaped

Snare Drum Stretcher, brass. new goods, 25 cents each.

Musicians' Polished Brass Coat Buttons, with harps. 35 cents dozen.

United States Army Civil War Fifes, serviceable

Under the heading of "Drums, Musical Instruments, Etc." one could find Spanish military bugle cap pins for 15¢; U.S. Navy Battle Rattles, considered "rare relics" for $3.75; and old "battered and dented" army or navy bugles for $1. (From Francis Bannerman Sons catalog.)

Four

THE CONSTRUCTION YEARS, 1901–1918

In 1901, Francis Bannerman built the No. 1 Arsenal for storage. Shortly after, he seized a publicity opportunity by putting the name of his business with the address of his store on the walls of the arsenal. Passengers on the passing boats and trains now saw his billboard.

By 1905, his business had grown dramatically. The catalog that was 20 pages in 1900, was now 132 pages. He needed to expand the arsenal. He also needed to improve his dock and build a harbor for lighters and barges.

His solution was to purchase underwater rights on the east and south sides of the island from the state of New York. The state stipulated that he mark his property line. He accomplished this by sinking old barges and boats on the east for the harbor and to the south for a breakwater. When the barges were filled with scraps from construction, he then built a walkway and entrance towers.

At the same time, his workers blasted down the rock on the south side of the No. 1 Arsenal to bring the grade down in order to construct the No. 2 and No. 3 Arsenals. Much of the rock created by the blasting was used to build the walls. Around this time he started to design with a castle in mind. The castle became one that is true Americana style because he took his influences from the castles of Europe, mostly from Scottish and Moorish structures.

In 1909, he designed and built the most distinctive part of the complex, the tower. This may have replaced a smaller one from 1905 that was in the space between the No. 2, and No. 3 Arsenals and the superintendent's house. He also started the family residence around this time. He and his wife Helen planted several gardens along the trail leading to the residence. The family home was perched on a high point in the center of the island looking down river towards West Point. Until his death in 1918, Bannerman continued to build by adding a lodge for workers and an icehouse. He also expanded the residence by enlarging it and adding a second floor.

Photographed in 1905 from the water to the north, this view shows the whitewashed No. 1 Arsenal with billboard information. The No. 3 Arsenal is being built between the No. 1 Arsenal and the superintendent's house. To the right, terrace walls of the Garden Brae near completion. (Courtesy of the Churchill/Bannerman family.)

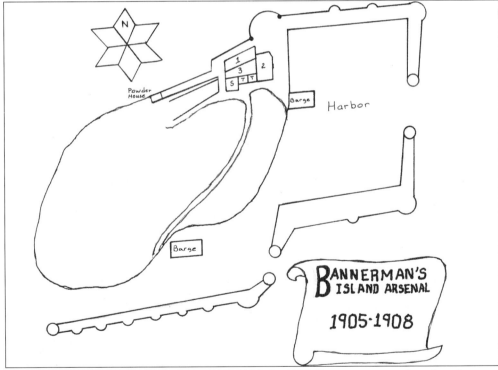

This plan shows what was built from 1905–1908. In 1905, Bannerman purchased underwater rights around the east and south side of the island. To mark his property line he sank barges and built a harbor and breakwater. At the same time he blasted the rock of the island down and built the No. 2 and No. 3 Arsenals. Trails were built and the arsenal started to look like a castle. (Plan by Thom Johnson.)

This drawing appeared on the rear cover of the 1907 Bannerman catalog. It shows the arsenal with a different tower. There is evidence on the inner wall of the ruins that it existed for a brief period. Bannerman used the arsenal as an advertisement and, realizing its attraction, he sold prints of it for 10¢.(From Francis Bannerman Sons July 1907 catalog.)

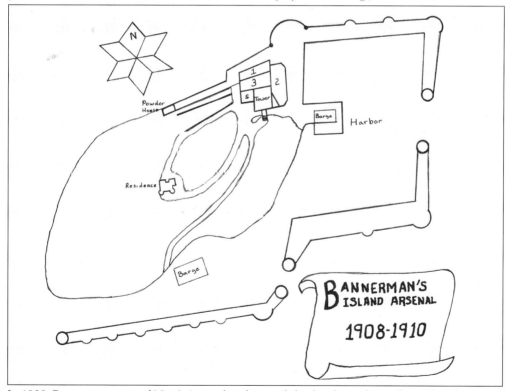

In 1908, Bannerman started No. 3 Arsenal and started the family residence, located at the center of the island looking south to West Point. During 1909, he built the tower possibly replacing one built earlier. The tower is the most distinctive part of the castle complex with all of its details and porches. Also finished at this time was the North Gate. (Plan by Thom Johnson.)

In this 1909 photograph, the tower (often referred to as "the castle") rises towards completion. Construction of the top floor has not yet begun. The lower picture shows another angle photographed from a boat entering the harbor. Bannerman's notes on the photograph point out locations for harbor towers and the Bannerman Island Arsenal sign. When completed, the tower would become the island's visual focal point. To this day, its walls entice gazes and wonderment from passersby in cars, trains, and boats. (Courtesy of the Churchill/Bannerman family.)

Viewed from the south east, this photograph shows the tower, the lodge, No. 2 Arsenal, and part of the dock. Close inspection shows a dock worker on the far left. (Courtesy of the Churchill/Bannerman family.)

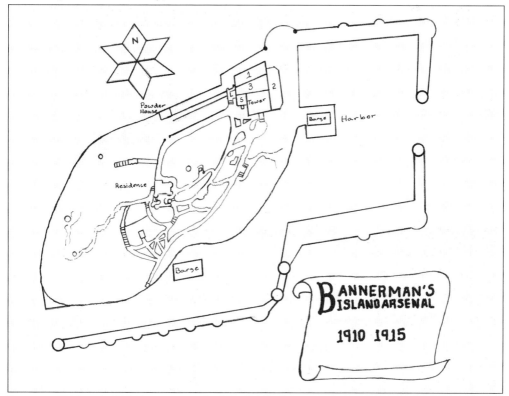

Between 1910 and 1915, Bannerman had built all of the storage space he needed. The arsenal was done. He then designed additions to the residence and, with his wife Helen, planned the gardens. It is likely this was also the time when the grotto, spring house, and out house were built. According to the date cast on the bridge of the Twin Towers it was built in 1912. The area at the Wee Bay is dated 1915. (Plan by Thom Johnson.)

The north arm of the harbor is undergoing construction in this photograph. Note the workers standing on the top of a "semi-tower," a term used by Bannerman in the plans he drew for the harbor. It is unknown what these semi-towers looked like when completed. This is one of the few photographs that show them at all. (Courtesy of the Churchill/Bannerman family.)

This photograph shows the completed lodge and sally port. This photograph may have been shot by Francis Bannerman or one of his sons. It is from one of the few negatives still owned by his family. (Courtesy of the Churchill/Bannerman family.)

This is a view of the lodge being built around 1916. On the top of the white part of the lodge one of the men is working on the third floor. Also note the men lined up on the dock. The bastion below the Bannerman name on the wall is different from what would eventually be built after the sally port was completed. (Courtesy of the Churchill/Bannerman family.)

On the left are the Twin Towers. Bannerman had many cannons placed as decorations both on the island and on the harbor arms. This cannon and large ball were among many found around the harbor. (Courtesy of Jane Bannerman.)

Photograph from the "Sundial" path, this view shows the east side of the residence. The section of the building with the four square windows was used as a dressing area and would be removed in later years when Bannerman built a dining room in its place. The second floor was also built at that time. (Courtesy of the Churchill/Bannerman family.)

This south view of the residence clearly shows the family coat of arms and the picture window with its scenic view down river. In the legend, under the coat of arms is the inscription "Crag Inch Lodge," which was the name Bannerman gave to the residence. Crag Inch means "rocky island." (Courtesy of the Churchill/Bannerman family.)

This photograph shows the front entrance to the residence. The residence is shown before the second floor extension was added. Note the wooden board on the left hand side of the picture. This was probably used as a path to make the uphill climb easier. (Courtesy of the Churchill/Bannerman family.)

Taken from below, this photograph of the west side of the residence shows how small it was at the time. The second floor and west extension were not yet built. Note the rocky terrain, a feature found throughout the island. (Courtesy of the Churchill/Bannerman family.)

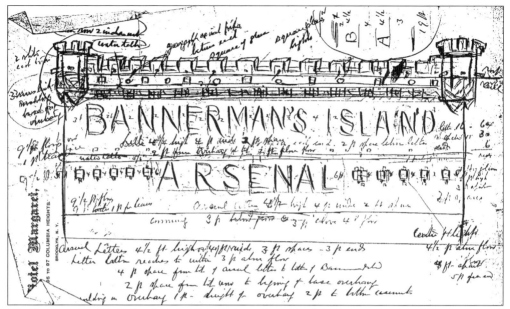

The Bannerman family lived at the Hotel Margaret in Brooklyn for many years. This drawing of the north side of the No. 3 Arsenal was drawn on the hotel's stationery. Among the specifications were four and one half foot high letters separated by three feet of space. The photograph was taken in recent times as indicated by the collapsed wall of the No. 1 Arsenal. This was the best photograph replicating the above drawing. (Above, courtesy of the Hagley Museum and Library; below, photograph by Thom Johnson.)

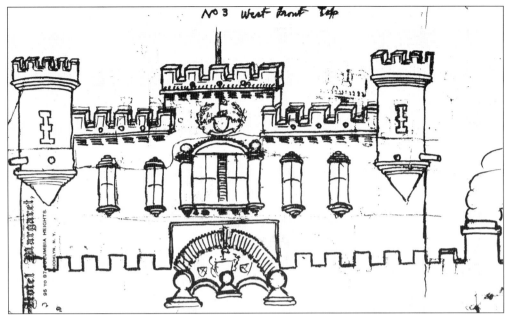

The drawing by Francis Bannerman VI was given to his workers to build the No. 3 Arsenal's west wall. He used a photograph of a fortification's gateway from Antwerp, Belgium as a reference. The masons did a wonderful job of taking the plan and turning it into a reality. The photograph shows the finished product. (Above, courtesy of the Hagley Museum and Library; below, courtesy of the Churchill/Bannerman family.)

This drawing by Bannerman shows most of his plan for the sally port. In it are the lodge to the left, the drawbridge and portcullis in the center, and the No. 2 Arsenal. Behind the entrance is his design for the arch leading to the tower. Sally ports are closely guarded openings or doors in the walls of a fortified building. Bannerman referred to the area around the portcullis (a heavy gate that could be lowered to bar the gateway) as his sally port. This made sense given that this was the business side of the island with the dock and storage nearby. Note the capstan and its platform, which created a nice centerpiece upon entering the island. To the left is the lodge and the No. 2 Arsenal is on the right. (Above, courtesy of the Hagley Museum and Library; below, courtesy of the Churchill/Bannerman family.)

Numerous spots for sitting and meditating could be found throughout the island. Francis Bannerman's sketch of a large sitting area is depicted here. The photograph was taken a number of years after its completion judging by the deterioration. On one of the steps it reads "Stop-Rest" with the date of 1911 and the initials "F. B." Inscribed on the seating area is a compass. (Above, courtesy of the Hagley Museum and Library; below, courtesy of the Churchill/Bannerman family.)

Taken around 1920, this picture shows the front of the superintendent's house. The entrance to the house originally faced north. But when Bannerman built the No. 3 Arsenal, the entrance had to be moved. In front of the house was a courtyard with an area for decorative plantings. (Courtesy of the Churchill/Bannerman family.)

Looking down to the sally port from under the arches, this view shows the working parts for the drawbridge and portcullis. Careful examination will show the capstan and the main dock. (Courtesy of the Churchill/Bannerman family.)

The final additions to the residence are shown in this 1918 photograph. On the west side of the house, Bannerman added an extension with a sun porch on ground level and a sleeping porch above. Between the pillars below the residence are steps leading to the grotto. (Courtesy of the Churchill/Bannerman family.)

Entrance West Breakwater with Twin Tower Bridge in distance

Pictured is the entrance to the breakwater. In the background are the Twin Towers. The Margaret Tower is to the right. A careful look at the island shows that walls are being built opposite the tower. This area marked the boundary of the Bannerman underwater rights. (Courtesy of the Churchill/Bannerman family.)

West Breakwater Portal Tower – Capt Andrew Nelson in motor Boat "IAN" (John)

At the end of the south breakwater sits the solitary Margaret Tower. Written at the bottom of this postcard view is "West Breakwater Portal Tower," an alternate name. Capt. Andrew Nelson stands in the Bannerman motor boat *Ian*. (Courtesy of the Churchill/Bannerman family.)

This will give view of Towers

This view shows the inside of the harbor's Twin Towers in 1912. These structures created a bridge from the south arm of the harbor to the south breakwater. On the original plan for this part of the complex, there was to be no bridge, just the two towers. (Courtesy of the Churchill/Bannerman family.)

The Twin Towers are shown in this photograph during the summer. The trees are in full bloom and the two towers look quite new. (Courtesy of the Churchill/Bannerman family.)

Looking east from the lodge one can see the Gap Towers. The Gap Towers mark the entrance to the island harbor. In the distance, a freight train can be seen going past the island. (Courtesy of the Churchill/Bannerman family.)

This is the rampart at the residence looking southeast. The cannon is from the Civil War. Just off to the left of the cannon under the cement is one of the four cisterns built to hold rainwater. The island had little drinking water on it so it was necessary to either bring water from the mainland or capture and store rainwater. (Courtesy of the Churchill/Bannerman family.)

A group of boys from New York City are having a wonderful time courtesy of Frank Bannerman. The boys enjoyed swimming, boating, fishing, and hiking in the fresh air. On the back of this photograph was written "Lining up for the start of the race." (Courtesy of the Churchill/Bannerman family.)

Francis Bannerman and family join the boys for dinner. The meal would invariably be topped off with homemade ice cream. Note the thistle pattern near the ceiling. The thistle was used by the early Scots as a warning against invaders. They would fill their dry moats with thistles. When their barefooted enemies approached they would be warned by their screams as they crossed the thistle-filled moat.(Courtesy of the Churchill/Bannerman family.)

The *Polopel* (on right) gets ready to depart the island for New York City. Aboard are the boys who have just spent some happy times on the island. The boat in the foreground is the *Eleanor*, owned by Daniel Carver of Newburgh, a friend of the family. (Courtesy of the Churchill/Bannerman family.)

This view of the main dock area shows the No. 2 Arsenal in the rear. On the lower left is the capstan from the *Wabash*. Behind it sits 18 six-inch U.S. Navy guns and two Bannerman presentation guns ready for loading on the lighter. The worker in the background is applying the Bannerman crest to a cannon. (Courtesy of the Churchill/Bannerman family.)

It is unknown why Bannerman had all these flags flying around the flag pole. The shot can be dated to early 1916 because it shows the rock of the island being blasted out and a grade being built for the sally port and lodge. To the right is part of a barge that was sunk in the center of the main dock. (Courtesy of the Churchill/Bannerman family.)

This six-inch cannon is ready to be loaded on the lighter. Note the growth of the trees along the harbor breakwater in the background. (Courtesy of the Churchill/Bannerman family.)

The picture's caption states "Hoisting gun and mounts on the lighter. 12 guns in 2 hours." Francis Bannerman's initials follow. In the background is one of the Gap Towers. (Courtesy of the Churchill/Bannerman family.)

A worker stands next to a barge loaded with crutches for a French hospital. According to the writing on the photograph the Bannerman company shipped 1,440 of them. (Courtesy of the Churchill/Bannerman family.)

Francis Bannerman gave freely and was very supportive of the Allies during World War I. Workers pose on a barge loaded with military clothing destined for Belgium in 1918. (Courtesy of the Churchill/Bannerman family.)

In this scene the barge of Belgium war relief clothing is being pulled out of the harbor by the Bannerman boat the *Polopel*. Note that the flag flying over the No. 3 Arsenal is not American, but is most likely Belgian. (Courtesy of the Churchill/Bannerman family.)

Bannerman is pictured here with his grandchildren, Frances and Donald. With his sleeves rolled up and his shoes dirty, he looked like a proud worker. Perhaps he had just built some steps so his family could better explore the island. (Courtesy of the Churchill/Bannerman family.)

The rampart by the residence provided a popular camera spot for the Bannermans. Walter and Anna Bannerman stand by the cannon during their summer vacation in 1916. Their three children, pictured from left to right, are Donald, Frances, and Dorothea. (Courtesy of the Churchill/Bannerman family.)

David (left) and Charles Bannerman pose at the rampart in front of a Civil War cannon that pointed down river towards West Point. (Courtesy of Jane Bannerman.)

Francis Bannerman was very proud of his Scottish heritage and his link to the MacDonald clan. This foundation stone, located on the exterior wall of the residence, is now safely in the possession of his great-granddaughter Ann Bannerman. (Courtesy of the Churchill/Bannerman family.)

This photograph shows the view of the grotto from the garden at Wee Bay. It is easy to see the stairs from below the residence to the grotto. Bannerman created many such places for rest and contemplation. Also note that the 1918 extension with sleeping porch and a sun porch had not yet been built. (Courtesy of the Churchill/Bannerman family.)

The living room furniture was simple but well made. Over the fireplace, cast into the plaster, read the inscription "Jehovah is my strength and shield." Similar inscriptions would be found throughout the house. (Courtesy of the Churchill/Bannerman family.)

This photograph shows the sun and sleeping porches of the residence. This was the last part of the complex that Bannerman designed and built in 1918, shortly before he died. This addition was very similar to the architectural style of Antoni Gaudi. Given that Bannerman was a world traveler, it is very possible that Gaudi was a reference for this design. (Courtesy of the Churchill/Bannerman family.)

With the gun dock in the foreground, this view shows the south side of the castle complex. Behind the dock are the lodge and the No. 2 Arsenal in the rear. The tower is at the high point. Note the four flags Bannerman had flying on that day. Many of the flag poles located throughout the island became lightning rods of sorts. Eventually the poles were not replaced. (Courtesy of the Churchill/Bannerman family.)

Bannerman's Island, Newburgh Bay, Hudson River, N. Y.

This postcard shows the island in its full glory. The breakwater in the foreground served as a nice promenade. Oddly enough, the postcard calls the island "Bannerman's Island" even though its official name remains Pollepel to this day. Close inspection of the shore to the right, reveals the lettering used to advertise the business. (Courtesy of Gary Ferguson.)

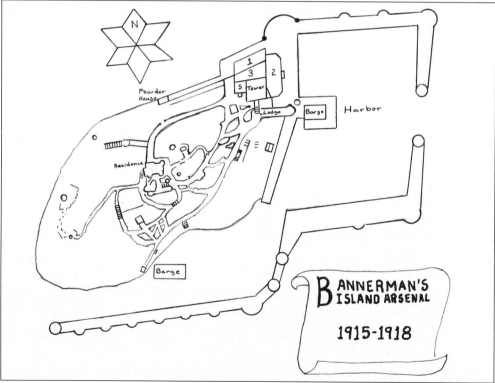

The final additions to the island complex were completed between 1915 and 1918. Starting in 1915, Bannerman built the lodge and sally port south of the No. 2 Arsenal. The gun dock and icehouse were built south of the lodge. The sleeping porch and sun porch were added to the west side of the residence. Bannerman had plans for two other projects; a mausoleum at the Garden Brae and a large gate at the Wee Bay. (Plan by Thom Johnson.)

Five

THE ISLAND WORKERS

In 1901, construction of the superintendent's house had begun. Obviously Bannerman deemed this a priority as he needed a trustworthy, reliable, knowledgeable individual to oversee day-to-day operations on the island, particularly during his frequent absences. In addition to running the business primarily out of New York City, Bannerman made frequent trips throughout the country and abroad to attend auctions and to meet with business contacts. Not one to waste a moment of his waking hours, Bannerman, judging from his diaries, also enjoyed playing the role of tourist during his excursions.

Jim Small would be the island's first superintendent. The superintendent's house, thereafter, was usually referred to as "Jim's house." One of Jim's faithful employees was Salvatore Scalzo, an immigrant from Calabria, Italy. Salvatore was hired at $1.35 per week, 10¢ more than his previous job at a local brickyard. Scalzo worked for the Bannermans for 14 years as a foreman and gardener. Other superintendents to follow included Charlie Kovac and Frank Crawford. Crawford, and his able assistant Wayne Owen, lived on the island and managed to raise their families there. Owen's daughter Phyllis was the only child to be born on the island. Crawford's tenure as superintendent lasted about 35 years when, in 1957, he retired due to poor health.

During the construction years of 1901 to 1918, and with the business growing, upwards of 40 people on any given day would be found on the island involved in a myriad of chores. Masons, carpenters, dock men, boat crews, guards, gardeners, warehouse workers, and family members probably created a climate of beehive proportions.

With each new step of construction, Bannerman would present his plans for the buildings and all of their ornate intricacies in the form of sketches he drew, often on hotel stationery or on the back of envelopes. When visiting the island, Bannerman would check the progress of his "blueprints." If not completely satisfied, he would order the workers to tear their work down and start over.

Even though the island had outlived its business usefulness by 1959, Charles Bannerman hired Joseph "Clem" Moshier to keep an eye on the remaining surplus of goods.

Helen Bannerman, second from left, stands with island workers and an unidentified woman on the back terrace of the residence. (Courtesy of the Churchill/Bannerman family.)

Workers prepare to move a cannon for shipment. In the picture below, note the three soldiers on the right assisting the island workers. They may have been present there as part of the government's investigation into the island's activities during World War I. Although eventually cleared of any wrongdoing, Bannerman, a very proud man, felt that his character and integrity were being taken into question. These events may have taken a toll on his health. (Courtesy of the Churchill/Bannerman family.)

Workers put finishing touches on the fireplace on the third floor of the lodge. This floor was also known as the Garden Brae. The lodge would be used to house employees for many years. (Courtesy of the Churchill/Bannerman family.)

Charles Kovac, believed to be pictured here with his wife in front of the sally port, served as superintendent for a number of years. His tenure was not without controversy. (Courtesy of the Bannerman Castle Trust.)

UNITED STATES OF AMERICA.

APPLICATION FOR PAROLE OF *Austrian* ALIEN ENEMY.

No. P._____

The application must be in duplicate and accompanied by three unmounted photographs of the applicant, not larger than 3 by 3 inches in size, which must be attached to this application. The photographs must be on thin paper and should have a light background. All should be signed by the applicant across the face of the photograph, so as not to obscure the features, if the applicant is able to write.

I, *Charles Kovac*, at present of *Storm King, Dutchess Co. N.* do hereby declare that I am at present a native, citizen, denizen, or subject of the *Austrian* Empire.

I hereby apply for parole or exemption temporarily from detention or deportation as a *Austrian* alien enemy under the proclamation of the President of the United States of America, dated _____ and in consideration of the granting of such temporary exemption I do hereby undertake and solemnly promise on my personal honor that I will carefully observe the laws of the United States of America and such regulations or orders as may be proclaimed and established for the conduct of alien enemies; and that I will strictly abstain from doing any act of hostility or injury to the United States and its people in any manner; that I will furnish a responsible person who is a citizen of the United States of America and who shall be acceptable to the authority granting my parole, to act as my supervisor; that I will keep in close touch with my supervisor and report in person to him as often as may be required; that I will report in person to any designated officer as often as may be required; that I will remain within the limits of my parole, to wit:

Southern District of New York including Dutchess County keep off all piers water fronts and not engage in any maritime or Governmental occupation

and that I will furnish a bond to insure my faithful performance of these obligations in the sum of $_____.

I understand that if I break this solemn promise my act will endanger all the privileges that may be extended to my countrymen in the United States and subject me to arrest, imprisonment, or deportation, also to punishment under the criminal laws of the United States, including treason, the punishment for which is death.

(Signed) *C. K.*
(Signature of applicant.)

SUPERVISOR'S AGREEMENT.

I, *F. B.*, of the city of *New York*
501 Broadway
(Street and number.)
State of *N.Y.*, being a citizen of the United States of America and engaged in the business of *Military Goods*
_____, hereby agree to act as supervisor over *Charles Kovac*, the maker of the above application for parole or exemption, to keep in close touch with him, and to promptly report any failure of the applicant to keep the conditions of his parole.

(Signed) *F. B.*
(Signature of supervisor.)

PAROLE.

Application granted, subject to revocation at any time if the Attorney General shall deem that the interests of the United States so require. Applicant shall report to his supervisor, once every *week*, and to the *Postmaster of Fy* in *Dutchess Co.* every *two weeks*. This parole will not be effective until bond for $ *250.00 in Liberty Bonds* is furnished.

May 13th 1918
(Date.)

Wm Wallace Jr c.p.a.
(Paroling authority.)
SPECIAL ASSISTANT TO THE ATTORNEY GENERAL

Charles Kovac, an Austrian-born superintendent for Bannerman, was arrested on the island on April 19, 1918. The arrest was ordered by the Navy Intelligence Bureau, which had been conducting an investigation into activities on the island during World War I. Despite Bannerman's total cooperation with authorities and his record for aiding the Allies, an exhaustive search of the island was undertaken. Among their findings, the investigative team found four machine guns mounted in the tower, which aroused their suspicion. At his hearing in New York City, Kovac stated that the guns were all second-hand and had been fired only to salute passing river steamers. Subject to deportation, Kovac was instead approved for parole. As noted in the document, Kovac's restrictions were delineated and Bannerman was required to sign off as his employee's supervisor. A letter written on June 19, 1918, to Franklin D. Roosevelt, Acting Secretary of the Navy, outlined Bannerman's objections to the occupation of the island. Eventually this led to his total exoneration. After gall bladder surgery, Bannerman's death on November 26, 1918, may have been hastened by his concerns about the accusations and the urgency of the Belgium Relief effort. (Courtesy of the Hagley Museum and Library.)

Looking across from the dock, workers drag materials across the ice. Although the ice presented obstacles, it also had its benefit. Charlie Crawford, son of superintendent Frank Crawford, tells a story of his father walking across the river's solid ice from the island to Beacon to obtain groceries and supplies. To fight the bitter cold, he would dress in many layers of clothing and wrap his legs and upper body with burlap tied in place with string. Frank Crawford poses in front of a Bannerman vessel. Charlie stands behind the boat. (Courtesy of the Churchill/Bannerman family.)

Leonard Wayne Owen is shown here standing on the roof of the tower. Referred to as Wayne, Owen served as assistant superintendent on the island for many years. After marrying Marion Scott in 1931, they would continue to live on the island with their four children for 10 more years. Wayne Owen passed away in 1995. Marion Owen died in 2003. (Courtesy of the Leonard Owen family.)

Seen here is Wayne Owen standing at the top of the "over and under the arches" stairs. The workers called it that because they could go under the stairs to the dock or over the stairs to the main entrance of the tower. (Courtesy of the Leonard Owen family.)

Marion Owen, Wayne's wife, with daughter Eleanor are seen here. The other Owen children were Leonard, Victor, and Phyllis. (Courtesy of the Leonard Owen family.)

Seen here is Eleanore Owen Seeland, one of Wayne Owen's children who grew up on Pollepel Island. She is riding her tricycle near the superintendent's house. (Courtesy of the Leonard Owen family.)

Payroll week ending Mar 22 including work on boat in city

Charlie	8.65
Joe	4.98
Fred	4.98
August	9.00
Jenkins	4.50
FB Jr	25.00
	$57.11

MAR 26 1902

Francis Bannerman submitted payroll statements typically on scraps of paper. (Courtesy of the Hagley Museum and Library.)

A sailor poses next to the cannon rack by the No. 2 Arsenal. A pile of large ordnance is nearby. (Unknown photographer.)

Six

HELEN BANNERMAN AND SONS

After the death of Francis Bannerman VI the business and arsenal passed to his wife Helen and sons Frank VII and David. The island continued to be used for storage. Goods were still shipped to and received from the island. Helen would spend the warm weather months on the island, but construction came to an end.

A major event occurred on August 15, 1920, when the powder house exploded. The force of the explosion sent a section of wall on to the New York Central Railroad tracks. Since many windows were blown out and not repaired, the elements were soon to affect the condition of the floors. Thus began the slow decline of the arsenal.

After Helen Bannerman's death in 1931, the island was used less frequently by the family. Maintenance was cut to a minimum. As the years passed, the gardens grew wild and the buildings started to decay.

There were times during this period when the family did visit and care for the castle. Jane C. Bannerman remembers spending a weekend at the residence cleaning up, possibly as preparation for the sale of the island. The arsenal was still filled with an amazing selection of stock for sale.

In the 1940s the sons, nearing retirement age, looked into selling the business and the island complex. With no takers, the firm continued to run. In 1945, Frank VII passed away. David was then joined by his sons, Charles and David Jr., to keep the business running.

In 1955, the 28th edition of the catalog was published. At this point it was common for an item to no longer have a price, a sign that it was no longer for sale but remained in the catalog merely as a reference for collectors. In 1957, David passed away and the business and arsenal became the responsibility of Charles, David Jr., and the family.

Helen Bannerman poses on the south side of the residence. The view down river was, and still is, spectacular. (Courtesy of the Churchill/Bannerman family.)

This picture shows Helen Bannerman hosting camp girls. The girls are picking flowers. (Courtesy of the Churchill/Bannerman family.)

Frank Bannerman VII (right) and his brother David Boyce Bannerman (below) became partners in their father's business in 1900. They served the business until their deaths, Frank in 1945 and David in 1957. The third son, Walter, became a doctor and practiced medicine in Massachusetts. (From Francis Bannerman Sons catalog.)

This cartoon was first published in *Life* magazine in 1922 and made light of the Bannerman second-hand military goods business. Given that it was published four years after Francis VI died, one of his sons would be the Mr. Bannerman who is off to camp. (From Francis Bannerman Sons 1920s catalog.)

This view of the harbor shows the whole castle complex. The No. 2 Arsenal is in front, covered in vines. Behind it, with the words Bannerman's Island Arsenal, is the whitewashed No. 3 Arsenal. The tower can be clearly seen in the background. The lodge, to the lower left, is also almost completely covered in vines. (Courtesy of the Bannerman family.)

This is the south side of the tower. Note the Bannerman coat of arms at the top of the building. In the ribbon under it was the inscription "*Pro deo et patria signum sustinemus,*" Latin for "we uphold the standard for God and country." Just below the ribbon, between the date (AD 1908), "Crag Inch Tower" was inscribed. (Courtesy of the Churchill/Bannerman family.)

These "sailors" are the children of David Bannerman, Francis VI's son. From left to right they are Alice, Charles, Margaret, and David Jr. This photograph was taken in Blue Point, Long Island, where the company moved after closing down Pollepel Island. (Courtesy of the Churchill/Bannerman family.)

A few young people are walking in line through the portcullis towards the east dock. (Courtesy of the Churchill/Bannerman family.)

The unidentified women in this picture are wearing pith helmets. They are standing at the North Gate of the island. (Courtesy of the Churchill/Bannerman family.)

David Bannerman Jr. is shown here on the main dock. Behind him is the east entrance to the No. 2 Arsenal. (Courtesy of the Churchill/Bannerman family.)

This view was taken from the top of the hill looking down to the Twin Towers at Wee Bay. Wee Bay is an area at the foot of the hill, below the residence, where Francis and Helen Bannerman created a formal pie-shaped garden. This photograph shows the incredible view of the Hudson River. It shows Breakneck Ridge to the left and Storm King Mountain to the right. Straight ahead is West Point. (Courtesy of the Churchill/Bannerman family.)

Prior to the explosion the powder house sat on the north side of the island at the end of the terrace wall where the Bannerman's had planted beautiful gardens. Note how the small building too had castle-like features. On August 15, 1920, the building exploded, throwing the door into the shallow water to the north. (Courtesy of the Churchill/Bannerman family.)

The powder house explosion of August 15, 1920, occurred when approximately 200 pounds of black powder combusted and spewed rock, shell fragments, and other material for great distances. Accounts have it that the explosion could be heard as far north as Poughkeepsie and as far south as Peekskill, a distance of almost 50 miles. Note the windows blown out. The castle complex suffered some structural damage as well. The residence was similarly affected. The force even blew some interior doors off their hinges. Some windows in nearby towns were shattered by the resounding blast. The powder house was located on the northwestern shore of the island near where the present day dock is located. No fatalities resulted from the blast. Helen was lucky enough to have just left from her rest in a hammock outside the residence to fetch a drink. The explosion flung a chunk of rock into the hammock while she was inside. Not one to shirk responsibility, the frail Helen then assisted with the impromptu bucket brigade to extinguish the island's fires. It was a landmark event in that the castle complex would never be quite the same again. (Courtesy of the Hagley Museum and Library.)

These women are having a mock sword fight at the top of the "over and under the arches" staircase leading into the tower. Note the pith helmets they have on. The Bannerman inventory included thousands of these helmets. (Courtesy of the Churchill/Bannerman family.)

The coat of arms that Francis Bannerman VI created for his family is clearly shown in this photograph of the residence. In the upper left hand corner is a ship and eagle depicting the MacDonald coat of arms. Below that is a grappling hook, which Francis once used to dredge material from the Brooklyn Harbor. In the upper right hand corner and also above the coat of arms, is a hand holding a banner. Francis told the story that his family came from the MacDonald clan of Scotland. One of his ancestors rescued the flag and gave it to King Robert the Bruce. The king tore off a piece and gave it back to the man naming him "the banner man." The lower right shows an ordnance pot. Under the coat of arms are the words "Crag Inch Lodge." *Crag Inch* is "rocky island" in Scottish. The lower photograph shows an original coat of arms, which was rescued by the family. It is now in the possession of Francis Bannerman's granddaughter. In all likelihood it came from the residence. (Above, courtesy of the Churchill/Bannerman family; below, photograph by Thom Johnson.)

Seven

The Decline and the Shutdown

After David Bannerman died in 1957 the business passed to his sons Charles and David Jr. Both men had other professions and were not prepared to head the firm. Needing a qualified person to run the day to day operations, longtime employee James (Jim) Hogan was promoted.

James Hogan was an army veteran who served with distinction during World War II. When he returned from the service, he was hired to pack and ship orders from the catalog. As the years progressed his knowledge and experience became invaluable to the firm. Eventually he rose in the business, purchased into it, and became its vice president.

Also in 1957, Charles Bannerman and James Hogan incorporated the business. They started to plan many needed changes. The island had become a bit of a problem given that methods of transportation had changed. Shipping gave way to trucking and the harbor had silted in. Lack of maintenance and the effects of the explosion in 1920 left parts of the arsenal in poor shape. Hence they needed to deal with a large stock of deteriorating ammunition, much of it very old.

In addition, the store at 501 Broadway had aged and become run down. The upper floors, where Francis Bannerman's museum was located, were no longer open to the public. Thus, changes to both the island and the store were necessary.

A new storage arrangement and store built at Blue Point on Long Island started the changes. The store at 501 Broadway was closed with its remaining stock sent to Blue Point. In 1958, arrangements were made for Val Forgett, a munitions expert, to safely dispose of all ordnance from the arsenal. Jim Hogan then organized workers to remove and send all good stock to Blue Point. Once this was done, the Smithsonian Institute was permitted to take any of the remaining stock.

By the early 1960s the island was to have few visitors. The superintendent now lived off the island and, at times, it was unattended. The visitors were mostly uninvited—boaters, some harmless collectors, photographers, and vandals. Time and tide were running out. The dock and harbor were breaking up from the winter freezes and the roof of the tower had partially collapsed. The Bannerman family looked to sell the island.

Jim Hogan is seen here in a boat with the castle in the background. Hogan worked for the Bannermans for many years at the 501 Broadway store. By the late 1950s, he had become the general manager and vice president. It became his responsibility to organize the clean up of the arsenal. (Photograph by Edward P. Seiss.)

One of the workers in the No. 2 Arsenal is preparing to look for usable stock. In the crates in front of him are leather goods including belts. In the foreground on top of a crate is a World War I helmet. (Photograph by Edward P. Seiss.)

Inside the No. 2 Arsenal, workers pick and stack goods to be shipped to Blue Point, the new storage and sales location. Note the condition of the lumber that makes up the roof. The wood that Francis Bannerman used to build these floors was recycled from the barges used to build the harbor. (Photograph by Edward P. Seiss.)

This is one of the lower floors inside of the tower. The old crates and wheels on the floor were viewed by many people at the time as old junk. To the collector of military goods, they were treasures. (Photograph by Edward P. Seiss.)

This view is of one of the top floors of the tower. In the upper left corner of the photograph is a section of the floor from above that had collapsed. The collapse was inevitable given that recycled material was used in the structures. In addition, the powder house explosion of 1920 exposed the upper floors to the elements. (Photograph by Edward P. Seiss.)

It is truly unfortunate that vandals gained access to the residence and smashed the picture window and what was left of the furniture. The lettering over the window and fireplace have survived. (Photograph by Edward P. Seiss.)

When Val Forgett took the challenge of cleaning the ordnance off the island he needed assistance. In this photograph, Forgett, shirtless on the left, is holding part of a limber. Note the workers wearing pith helmets. These came from the arsenal's stock. (Courtesy of Val Forgett III, Val Forgett collection.)

This photograph shows the ordnance yard outside the No. 1 and No. 2 Arsenals. Forgett and his workers have stacked and organized cannon balls and shells in preparation for their shipment off the island and eventual disposal. (Courtesy of Val Forgett III, Val Forgett collection.)

Stacks of ammunition and other ordnance are being prepared before being loaded on the landing craft to the rear. This type of vessel was necessary for transportation because the harbor had silted in and only shallow draft vessels could enter. (Courtesy of Val Forgett III, Val Forgett collection.)

This Civil War caisson is on the main dock waiting to be shipped off the island. Considering it was about 100 years old at the time of this photograph, it was in very good condition and made quite a historical artifact. (Courtesy of Val Forgett III, Val Forgett collection.)

The small door at the bottom in the center was an entrance to one of the outhouses built into the complex. The only building on the island that had a toilet with running water was the Bannerman residence. (Photograph by Edward P. Seiss.)

The bottom floor of the lodge housed the generator. It provided electricity for the island. The generator was installed in the late 1920s, years after Francis Bannerman VI's death. (Courtesy of Val Forgett III, Val Forgett collection.)

Norman Hay (left) and Douglas Tietze are two of the lucky collectors who were with Mike Khantzian for one of the last clean ups on the island. Here they are looking at some of the items found in the arsenal. Even the wooden crate that once held a Hotchkiss gun would now be of interest to collectors. (Photograph by Mike Khantzian.)

In the center of this photograph looking at the camera is Clem Moshier. He was the last superintendent for the island and was supervising what was to be one of the last clean-ups of the arsenal. In the foreground are sacks filled with what appear to be leather goods including holsters and belts. (Photograph by Mike Khantzian.)

This is the east wall of the No. 1 Arsenal and provided the original entrance to the building. It had three large loading doors in the center, one for each floor. (Photograph by Mike Khantzian.)

The photographer is standing on top of the No. 2 Arsenal looking at the tower and No. 3 Arsenal. Many of the textures that Bannerman used on the top two floors can be seen. The brick is corbelled or laid past the plumb line. There is a rampart wall and half columns or pilasters. The little structure over the "A" in arsenal is called a crow's nest and breaks up the rampart quite well. (Photograph by Mike Khantzian.)

This view is from the roof of the lodge looking up at the top two floors of the tower. These two floors were the most decorated among the buildings Bannerman designed. Each of the four sides are similar but with minor variations. One architectural detail that is the same for each side are the porches at the top. At one point Gatling guns were mounted on each porch. (Photograph by Mike Khantzian.)

94

Looking straight up at the southeast corner of the tower an interesting architectural feature are the cylinders at the corners. They are corbelled so that the higher walls appear larger. Also note the metal basket and bracket. This is called a faggot burner and was used to burn bundled sticks and rags to illuminate the buildings at night. (Photograph by Mike Khantzian.)

The west walls of the tower, superintendent's house, and the entrance to the No. 3 Arsenal are photographed from the Garden Brae. Note the architectural details that are used on the top of the tower. There is no doubt that Bannerman liked to use the ball decoration. Along the rampart wall there are half balls and over the arch are full balls. (Photograph by Mike Khantzian.)

This photograph was taken from the north arm of the harbor looking at the east side of the castle. Bannerman designed most of the buildings without right angles. This created some interesting perspectives. Note that the north wall of the tower appears to go to a different vanishing point than that of the No. 2 Arsenal. The reason for this is that they are not parallel walls. (Photograph by Mike Khantzian.)

This excellent shot shows the tower and No. 2 Arsenal taken near the cannon storage area. At this point, the poison ivy is starting to cover the structure and many of the windows are broken. (Photograph by Mike Khantzian.)

This fireplace was in the dining room of the Bannerman residence. Note the "thanks" inscribed above it. One side of the fireplace is engraved with shamrocks, the other side with thistles, perhaps portraying the Irish and Scottish roots of the family. Along the fireplace are built-in cabinets. (Photograph by Mike Khantzian.)

Over the fireplace in the guest bedroom on the second floor of the residence, Bannerman wished for his guests to be sustained by Jehovah after having laid down to sleep. Jane Bannerman's father, Edward Campbell, once spent the night in this room. The man had a hard time sleeping because he was afraid the balls would fall and kill him in his sleep. (Photograph by Mike Khantzian.)

Helen Bannerman had an old fashioned pump organ in the sunroom of the residence. There she would play for family and friends and loved to entertain the children of the island workers. Sadly this photograph shows the organ in 1968 after vandals had destroyed this once proud tool of the musician. (Photograph by Mike Khantzian.)

The sally port is shown here in 1968. The island had a number of invited visitors. Mike Khantzian, a professional photographer from Fort Lee, New Jersey, was one of them. Khantzian, along with Dr. Halbert Fillinger, Norman Hay, and Douglas Tietze, visited to collect what was left of interest. Khantzian took these photographs of the complex a year before the fire. (Photograph by Mike Khantzian.)

Gerald Stowe, former curator of the West Point Military Museum, spent much time on the island. This photograph, taken in the mid-1960s, shows his sons Gerald Jr. on the left and Sheldon on the right standing at the drawbridge holding flashlights, probably used to explore the dark cavernous arsenal. (Courtesy of Sheldon Stowe.)

Eight

FROM ISLAND
TO PARKLAND

In the early 1960s, the Bannermans were faced with the difficult problem of what to do with the castle complex. Boats and barges able to serve the island were few and some could not enter the harbor because of silting. The buildings had many problems relating to deferred maintenance. The roof leaked and the floors were unsafe. The harbor was breaking up and becoming a submerged obstruction. The cost of keeping the island was becoming a liability.

The family tried finding another use for the island and the complex. David Jr., a naval architect, looked into the possibility of rebuilding the harbor to create a marina. However, it was determined that the cost of repairs for this scenario was too high and the prospects of success were uncertain. Even if the marina project was feasible, problems with the arsenal and residence needed addressing. Realistically they had no choice but to sell.

In 1965, a committee of conservationists began investigating the possibility of purchasing property along the Hudson River to be preserved as park land. This property included Pollepel Island. This proposal came at the ideal time for the Bannerman family, as it met their desire to sell the island. The Jackson Hole Preserve, a Rockefeller Foundation, provided $108,041 to purchase Pollepel Island. The title went from Francis Bannerman Sons Inc. to the People of the State of New York on December 28, 1967.

The island was off limits to the public because of the dangerous condition of the buildings. On August 8, 1969, a spectacular fire destroyed much of the buildings on the island. New York State troopers and firemen rowed out to the island to check if anyone may have been trapped on the island. Once they decided no one was there, they let the buildings burn since the intense heat made it impossible to fight. The cause of the fire was never determined. When the fire burned itself out, all that remained were the exterior walls of the castle complex.

This view on the island from the south east, shows the south breakwater, the Twin Towers, and the castle in the distance. (Courtesy of the Bannerman family.)

On August 8, 1969, at 12:40 a.m., a fire alarm was turned in to the New York State Police. The Bannerman Castle complex was ablaze. Two New York State troopers along with several Beacon firemen rowed to the island. The troopers quickly searched for persons possibly trapped on the island. The firemen stayed in the rowboat, helpless to fight the enormous blaze. The fire illuminated the night sky as the flames rose more than 100 feet above the castle's towers. The flames could be seen as far as Goshen. Due to the intense heat, no efforts were made to fight the fire. All that remained after the fire were the stone, cement, and brick walls of the building. The interior floors made from ships' planks, coated with creosote, were totally destroyed as were much of the wooden beams. Beacon firemen hosed the roof of the Dutchess Manor Restaurant and other buildings within a quarter mile to prevent the showering sparks from doing further damage. It is believed that the police investigated the possibility of arson, but no proof was found. (Unknown photographer.)

These photographs were taken around 1970. At the top, one can see the north Gap Tower with a "no trespassing" sign near a section of its collapsed wall. In the background, forsythia, Virginia creeper, and poison ivy continue their invasion of the main arsenal. Below are the sally port with the tower to the rear and the No. 2 Arsenal to the right. (Photograph by Edward P. Seiss.)

Pictured are the interiors of the No. 2 and No. 3 Arsenals. The photographer was standing in the south east corner of the No. 2 Arsenal. The wall that once proclaimed "Bannerman Island Arsenal" has partially collapsed leaving only a corner still standing. The bottom view shows the same wall from inside the No. 3 Arsenal. This wall is very unstable and it is understandable why this area is off limits to the public. (Photograph by Edward P. Seiss.)

This view looks into the No. 2 Arsenal shortly after the fire. The balls on the top of the rampart wall are ocean buoys that Bannerman used like finials on top of the buttresses. The windows to the left of the center of the photograph were arches. That area may have been the original entrances to the No. 2 Arsenal. (Photograph by Edward P. Seiss.)

Looking into the No. 3 Arsenal at the west wall, this photograph shows the massive stone wall that Francis Bannerman had built. The material used was created by blasting the island rock to make space for the arsenal. The section of wall on the fourth floor that is finished in concrete may have been an area that Bannerman used as an office. (Photograph by Edward P. Seiss.)

The sally port and tower are seen here after the fire. Note the empty spaces where there were once shields. These were removed by many different people over a period of years prior to the fire. (Photograph by Sheldon Stowe.)

This view shows the moat brae at the portcullis and the capstan. One related fact to the fire is that the portcullis, which was made of wood, survived the fire as this photograph shows. Vandals have destroyed what was left of the portcullis. (Photograph by Sheldon Stowe.)

This early 1970s image shows the west wall of the tower. The photograph shows all the details that were used on the tower. The turret to the right has, even to this day, a metal spiral stairway that goes to the top. Island workers once used this stairway to get to the roof. (Photograph by Sheldon Stowe.)

The south interior wall of the No. 2 Arsenal was built on fill that went into the Hudson River. As the walls settled they started to crack as can been seen in this photograph. (Photograph by Sheldon Stowe.)

This is an aerial view of the island complex from around 1930. This clearly shows the harbor, breakwater, dock, and the island arsenal. (Photograph from *The Story of Bannerman Island*, by Charles S. Bannerman.)

An aerial photograph taken from the north east shows all of the odd angles that were used when building the storage facilities. The No. 3 Arsenal is in the foreground. Note the structure has a keystone shape. (Copyright 2001 Paul Harrington.)

Nine

THE BANNERMAN
CASTLE TRUST

Prior to the establishment of the Bannerman Castle Trust, plans for the island were uncertain at best. The New York State Office of Parks, Recreation and Historic Preservation had declared the island a "scenic ruin" and "off limits" to the public.

In 1993, the Bannerman Trust was organized in Brooklyn by Neil Caplan, Thom Johnson, Jane Bannerman, Susan Andersen, Dr. Sheila McManus, Robert McKenna, and Darlene Swann. After its inception a resolution was introduced by Dutchess County legislator John Ballo to change the status of the island and to support the trust's preservation efforts.

To bring attention to the island, members of the trust talked to community groups and gave lectures and slide shows promoting the island's preservation.

In 1994, the Bannerman Trust incorporated as a not-for-profit organization and its name changed to the Bannerman Castle Trust Inc. After Gov. George E. Pataki's appointment of Bernadette Castro as parks commissioner in 1995, the fate of the island changed. A meeting between Commissioner Castro and Jane Bannerman resulted in the trust becoming the official "friends" organization with the New York State Office of Parks, Recreation and Historical Preservation.

In the ensuing years, the trust has made many strides. An observation deck at Breakneck Ridge Whistle Stop was installed and a partnership was created with the tour boat *Pride of the Hudson*. A spectacular night illumination show of the arsenal was staged by Deke Hazirjian of New York City Lites in 1998. The island was opened to kayak hard hat tours and eventually, with the installation of a new dock and stairway, the trust opened the island to the public for boat trips and guided tours in the fall of 2003. Currently the tours depart Newburgh and Beacon from May through October each year. Bannerman historians lead the tours and relate the history and legends of the island.

The Bannerman Castle Trust Inc. continues to work towards its mission to create a master plan and eventually stabilize the island structures. It is hoped that visitors can enjoy it as a cultural, historical, and recreational facility for years to come.

Members of the Bannerman Castle Trust and New York State park employees from left to right are (first row) Bill Bauman and Francis Bannerman VIII; (second row) Jim Moogan, Neil Caplan, and Jane Bannerman; (third row) Thom Johnson standing in front of the tower. (Courtesy of the Bannerman Castle Trust.)

From left to right, Joan Pagones, town of Fishkill supervisor; Albert Romanelli, deputy mayor of Beacon; and Jane Bannerman cut the ribbon on the Bannerman Island Interpretive Sign in 2000. This sign is at an observation deck just north of Metro-North's Breakneck Ridge whistle stop. (Courtesy of the Bannerman Castle Trust.)

To promote and educate the public about the castle complex, the Bannerman Castle Traveling Sculpture was created. The three-dimensional "castle," built by local artist Kevin McCurdy, was funded in part by a grant from the New York State Council for the Arts. Visitors were able to walk inside the structure to view a variety of exhibits. (Courtesy of the Bannerman Castle Trust.)

Jim Logan, a former member of the Board of the Bannerman Castle Trust, is paddling his canoe past the north side of Bannerman's Island. Logan was very involved over the years bringing people to and from the island in his canoe. (Photograph by Thom Johnson.)

In order to raise money and awareness about the island the trust produced a cookbook. The cookbook included recipes and stories from people who had lived or worked on the island. Pictured above from left to right are (first row) Marion Owen and Isabel Scalzo; (second row) Jane Bannerman, Joan Pagones, and Evelyn Owen Palen holding copies of the book. (Courtesy of the Bannerman Castle Trust.)

On summer days, Francis Bannerman (standing wearing vest) frequently brought boys from his Brooklyn neighborhood to the island where they enjoyed boating, swimming, and fishing. The evenings would end with dinner and ice cream in the residence's dining room. This picture shows the Manly Boys Club posing for a group shot at the entrance to the residence. (Courtesy of the Churchill/Bannerman family.)

Coauthor Thom Johnson (upper left in white shirt) poses with a group of his art students from Irvington High School who visited the island to work on a school project. Note the location of Johnson relative to Bannerman in the above photograph. (Courtesy of Thom Johnson.)

On July 6, 2002, Bannerman Castle formed the backdrop to a special wedding uniting Billynda Kirshhoffer and Karl Baker. It was the island's first. A bagpiper entertained guests who remained aboard the reception boat the *Pride of the Hudson*. They were able to watch the ceremony through a video link. The trust has hosted other special events including a Fourth of July fireworks cruise, a catered banquet, a Halloween tour at dusk, and a hot apple pie and cider tour. (Photograph by Neil Caplan.)

Neil Caplan, Bannerman Castle Trust president, displays a rifle from the collection of Andrew Lustyik. The rifle once belonged to David Bannerman. (Photograph by Andrew Lustyik.)

Through the efforts of the Bannerman Castle Trust and John Lawrence, a dock and stairway were built to accommodate tour groups. Here the construction is in its final stages. Since 2003, visitors have been enjoying a pleasant informative cruise to the island aboard the *Pollepel* in preparation for their island tour. (Courtesy of the Bannerman Castle Trust.)

Like Francis Bannerman, the trust has used the island as a teaching tool for youngsters. Here Thom Johnson's students are landing on the island at Wee Bay. They would spend the day creating artwork and photographs. Bannerman would have been pleased. (Photograph by Thom Johnson.)

Walt Thompson, an avid kayaker, took this photograph when he came upon this scene in September 2000. Often boaters are unaware of the old harbor, which can be seen only at low tide. This powerboat got stuck in the harbor. Under the bow of the boat is a submerged obstruction marker placed by the Bannerman Castle Trust just 24 hours before the incident. (Photograph by Walt Thompson.)

EPILOGUE

It has been the goal of the authors to present in words, photographs, and art work the story of an American castle. The castle and the man who designed and built it are an important part of American history. Francis Bannerman VI saw greater value in his wares than simply scrap. He discovered that military goods had great value as history.

The book ends by presenting some of the changes that time has created. Unfortunately most changes have not been for the better. Vandals have destroyed many parts of the old walls and normal wear has also taken its toll. But with the Bannerman Castle Trust and two island stewards assigned by the New York State Department of Parks, Recreation and Historic Preservation to care for the castle, the uninvited visit less often, the trails are maintained, and there are guided tours of the island.

The authors also present a few photographs of what the island looks like now to show how beautiful it still is and why it still draws people. Come and visit.

In conclusion, readers might reflect on the man that was Francis Bannerman VI. His hard work led him to create the largest and most complete army-navy store. His business was so large that he needed an island arsenal. Readers also might think about his observation that there was historical value in the tools of the military. As proof of that philosophy, Bannerman created, at his store in New York City, a display area that he called the Museum of Lost Arts. His hope for the museum was that it would encourage people to study war so that the world would no longer have to practice it.

This 1968 view from the water clearly shows that the top two floors of the tower dominate the other parts of the structures. But it also shows how poison ivy and the tides are taking over the island. (Photograph by Mike Khantzian.)

Also from 1968, this photograph shows the intricate details on the top two floors. The exterior of these floors were the most decorated, but on the inside they were rarely used. The Crawford and Owen families and the island workers used the top floor to keep chickens. The floor below was used to stretch out fabric to make sails. (Photograph by Mike Khantzian.)

This view of the east wall of the tower shows the four and a half foot letters spelling "Bannerman's." The floor above was one of the only empty spaces in the castle. Wayne Owen's wife, Marion, told of how they had been given tennis balls and rackets. They used the space to play their own version of tennis. (Photograph by Mike Khantzian.)

The arched entrance to the tower from the top of the No. 2 Arsenal illustrates how Francis Bannerman used many balls as decorations. It is unknown why Bannerman used that detail so much. It could be an element from Moorish architecture that appealed to him for its meaning of nobility. (Photograph by Mike Khantzian.)

The west wall of the residence shortly after the fire is shown in this photograph. The window above the arch on the left was the bathroom. The cylinder to the right of the window contains one of the cisterns, or tanks, to hold rain water. Further to the right is the sleeping porch with the sun porch below. (Photograph by Sheldon Stowe.)

A grotto is a cavern or shelter. This column was built in to a rock overhang below the residence. Bannerman designed and built many places where the family and island visitors could sit and think. (Photograph by Sheldon Stowe.)

This photograph was taken shortly after the fire in 1969. It takes careful examination to see that the buildings are just shells with only the walls standing. One sad note about this photograph is that the wall, which says Island Arsenal (middle level of structures), would soon fall. (Photograph by Mike Khantzian.)

In this 1980s photograph, the beauty of the castle complex is evident in this winter scene. It is easy to understand why the glorious ruins are still visited and photographed by so many each year. (Photograph by Thom Johnson.)

The North Gate (the arched opening on the lower right) is clearly visible in this view taken from the north. Just to its left is what remained of the No. 1 Arsenal after the 1969 fire. The lettering on the north wall clearly states that this was Bannerman's Island Arsenal. (Photograph by Thom Johnson.)

The Twin Towers were connected by a bridge from the south arm of the harbor to the breakwater. This winter photograph shows the southern tower. It had a ladder to the top where there was a lovely sitting area with a beautiful down-river view of the Hudson Highlands. (Photograph by Thom Johnson.)

This view of the tower was taken from the old gun dock. The white wall of the lodge stands out and the different textures that Bannerman used can be seen. Note the rope pattern along the walls. This was also used on the harbor towers and was likely a reference to his sales of scrap rope as a young man. (Photograph by Thom Johnson.)

This is the south wall of the Bannerman residence shown in its heyday. The Bannerman Castle Trust would like to restore this structure so that it may be used once again. The building might be used to welcome visitors and to educate the public about Francis Bannerman's business and vision. (Courtesy of the Bannerman family.)

This scene was created with the help of lighting designer Deke Hazirjian and his company New York City Lights. In 1998, Hazirjian, in conjunction with the trust, helped sponsor an illumination of the arsenal. This image has often been confused with that of the 1969 fire. In fact, it illustrates how citizens of today have used the Bannerman Castle complex in creative ways. Hopefully, like a phoenix, the castle will rise again and find use as a recreational and educational resource. (Photograph by Thom Johnson.)

ACROSS AMERICA, PEOPLE ARE DISCOVERING SOMETHING WONDERFUL. THEIR HERITAGE.

Arcadia Publishing is the leading local history publisher in the United States. With more than 3,000 titles in print and hundreds of new titles released every year, Arcadia has extensive specialized experience chronicling the history of communities and celebrating America's hidden stories, bringing to life the people, places, and events from the past. To discover the history of other communities across the nation, please visit:

www.arcadiapublishing.com

Customized search tools allow you to find regional history books about the town where you grew up, the cities where your friends and family live, the town where your parents met, or even that retirement spot you've been dreaming about.